EDWARD DOUGLASS WHITE
LECTURE SERIES

Previously published
in the Edward Douglass White Lecture Series

R. M. MACIVER, *Leviathan and the People*

ROBERT M. HUTCHINS, *Education for Freedom*

EDWARD S. CORWIN, *Liberty Against Government*

PAUL H. APPLEBY, *Morality and Administration in Democratic Government*

LEONARD D. WHITE, *The States and the Nation*

JEFFERSON B. FORDHAM, *A Larger Concept of Community*

WALTER GELLHORN, *Individual Freedom and Governmental Restraints*

ALPHEUS T. MASON, *The Supreme Court from Taft to Warren*

ROBERT J. HARRIS, *The Quest for Equality*

ARTHUR LARSON, *When Nations Disagree*

FREDERICK L. SCHUMAN, *The Cold War: Retrospect and Prospect*

JEROME HALL, *Comparative Law and Social Theory*

WILLIAM A. ROBSON, *The Governors and the Governed*

PAUL G. KAUPER, *Religion and the Constitution*

KENNETH CULP DAVIS, *Discretionary Justice: A Preliminary Inquiry*

STRUCTURE AND RELATIONSHIP
IN CONSTITUTIONAL LAW

Structure and Relationship in Constitutional Law

CHARLES L. BLACK, JR.

LOUISIANA STATE UNIVERSITY PRESS   *Baton Rouge*

To Gavin and David Black

Preface

These lectures are printed just about as delivered at the Louisiana State University in March, 1968, as the Edward Douglass White Lectures on Citizenship.

I am deeply grateful to the Law School, the Department of Government, and the Graduate School, all at the Louisiana State University, for their kind invitation and for the innumerable courtesies which made my stay in Baton Rouge so pleasant. I am also grateful to Mrs. Amelie Gollinger, who did not in this case depart from her invariable practice of giving me such secretarial help as can almost make writing a pleasure. I am grateful, for courtesies and help, to Mr. Richard Wentworth, Director of the Louisiana State University, and to Mrs. Margaret Porter, the editor who worked with me on the manuscript. Thanks, as always, are owing to Barbara Aronstein Black, who read the manuscript as it formed and made valuable suggestions.

C. L. B., Jr.

Contents

STRUCTURE AND RELATIONSHIP
IN CONSTITUTIONAL LAW

I · Inference from Structure: The Neglected Method

In her principal work, an acknowledged classic of anthropology, the late Ruth Benedict developed and illustrated, to the fascination of millions of readers, the thesis that each human culture selects, from the comprehensive circle of possibility, only a few segments within which to develop its own modes of being, its own patterns.[1] Karl Llewellyn has made us keenly aware of those highly specific differences in legal styles that vary from culture to culture and from period to period.[2] I am going to talk, in these lectures, about a stylistic preference, or, perhaps better, a preference of intellectual method, of that part of our culture which we call constitutional law, with some illustrations both in experience and in possibility.

I think it well, before we begin exploring the intricacies of real legal life and thought, to state abstractly what I am going to be talking about. Perhaps I ought to set a frame of reference by reminding you

[1] THE PATTERNS OF CULTURE (1934).
[2] See, e.g., THE COMMON LAW TRADITION, pp. 35 ff. (1960).

of the basics of law-finding method as received among us. I am here referring not to the higher speculations of jurisprudence; I am interested, rather, in the thing that would probably most interest an anthropologist: What basic kinds of legal reasoning, broadly, does the ordinary, competent American judge see as being open to him when he has to ascertain and fix the right law for application to a case before him?

I ought to say, parenthetically, since I have the honor of speaking in this place, that I am not in any way a civilian, and that my generalizations may therefore be wrong or skewed for the civil law. But I think my approximation to the dominant American mode will be reasonably accurate as approximations go.

Most fundamentally, there are two great headings, corresponding to two bodies of material conceived by the working lawyer as formal sources of law. One is the method of precedent, the finding of sound analogy in the past case or line of cases. Out of the development of such decisional reasoning, systematic concepts develop, but the *case* remains paramount in importance and in authority. This is the heart-method of Anglo-American legal reasoning. But legislative activity, administrative rule-making, the conceiving of treaties as municipal law, and the making of written constitutions have brought into being in highly developed form a second and seemingly quite different method—the searching of the written text for its *meaning* in application to the presented case.

These are our two basic legal methods. They do not cover the whole circle of possibility. Reasoning from natural law principles, directly, has been recommended as a mode of choice.[3] Norway, in a manner perhaps fully understandable only by her own lawyers, has used custom, directly, as a source of law, sometimes overriding even concededly clear statutory and constitutional provisions.[4] On the other hand, the method of systemization from precedent—the classic method of the common law—is said not to play a central or even an explicit role in some other legal systems, though an American-trained lawyer finds it hard to conceive of its absence—just as an English-speaker finds it hard to conceive of languages in which tenses are not distinguished.

Our two dominant methods have come, further, into a distinctive and by no means logically necessary relation. The first method—the case method—is first in time and is clearly first in dominance, doubtless because the immemorial traditions of our legal training and professional lore have always stressed it. The systematic development of case law must, of course,

[3] See my *The Two Cities of Law* in THE OCCASIONS OF JUSTICE, p. 17 (1963).

[4] T. Leivestad, *Custom as a Type of Law in Norway*, 54 Law Quarterly Review 95, 266 (1938).

use this method. But there was no absolutely compelling reason for its extension into the field of textual interpretation, which today comprehends so many—perhaps most—of the legal problems tendered to the judiciary for solution. It would have been logically possible for our courts to have held themselves bound by the cases where the cases were the only source of law, while standing permanently and wholly free to reexamine questions of textual interpretation. That (naturally enough, when the thing is viewed as a matter of institutional behavior) is not what happened. Lawyers trained in the precedent system seem to have assumed that that system was to be employed when questions of statutory or constitutional construction were at bar. The case of authority fixes textual construction just as it fixes the common law. The consequence, as all know, is that the weathered and often litigated-under statute, or constitutional provision—or, for that matter, the weathered administrative regulation—comes often to be little more than a sort of heading for the cases decided under it; after a time, it is to these that practical lawyers look for law. I know lawyers who work most effectively on constitutional problems and who yet do not have at all clear in their minds the exact texts that they are, as a formal matter, working with. An argument about a ship's deviation, posed purely on the text of the

Carriage of Goods By Sea Act, is likely to irritate and bore law students; they feel it to be somehow irrelevant to the job of perceiving that act, whatever its own language, as an event placed in a stream of decisional law. Still, the new case of textual interpretation is common enough, and the formal assumption always remains that the precedent cited in a statutory or constitutional case is a precedent concerning the interpretation of a textual passage. This assumption not only plays its part in evaluation of precedent lines and in affecting the probability of overruling, but also tends to set the categories of the subject.

Now I have thus far refreshed your recollection on certain rather obvious things about our legal culture because I am going to concentrate on one thing within this field. Let me state my thesis at once. What I shall discuss is the great extent to which, in dealing with questions of constitutional law, we have preferred the method of purported explication or exegesis of the particular textual passage considered as a directive of action, as opposed to the method of inference from the structures and relationships created by the constitution in all its parts or in some principal part.

It would be intellectually satisfying, though the fact would be far from satisfying, to be able to say that our legal culture *never* employs, for constitutional

law, the method of inference from structure and relation, but always purports to move on the basis of
the interpretation of particular constitutional texts.
As we shall see, that is not true; the first of these styles
of thought has played its part at at least one point
of the very first importance in the development of
our constitutional law, and at other points of somewhat less importance. What can be asserted is that
our preference for the particular-text style has been a
decided one, leading not only to the failure to develop
a full-bodied case-law of inference from constitutional
structure and relation but even to a preference, among
texts, for those which are in form directive of official
conduct, rather than for those that declare or create
a relationship out of the existence of which inference
could be drawn.

I should like to begin with the case of *Carrington*
v. *Rash*, decided by the Supreme Court in 1965.[5]

Carrington was a career man in the United States
Army. He had enlisted at the age of eighteen, from
his then home in Alabama. Some seventeen years later,
at the time he brought his action, he was living in El
Paso, Texas, with his wife and two children, commut-
ing thence to his Army job and running a small
business on the side. He was paying property taxes in
Texas and was conceded by the state to be a bona fide

[5] 380 U.S. 89 (1965).

resident of El Paso County. Naturally enough, he wanted to vote. But the Texas constitution contained a provision, hardly open to interpretation, which would ban him from voting. It ran as follows: "Any member of the Armed Forces of the United States or component branches thereof, or in the military service of the United States, may vote only in the county in which he or she resided at the time of entering such service so long as he or she is a member of the Armed Forces." [6]

Carrington did not reside in El Paso County, or in any Texas county, at the time of his entering the service in 1946. Whether Alabama would still be willing to receive an absentee ballot from a son so long missing was questionable, and somewhat beside the point, for Carrington wanted to vote where his home was. Texas election officials, virtually constrained by this constitutional provision, refused him the vote, and he brought suit to get it. After an adverse decision in the Texas Supreme Court, he took his case to the Supreme Court of the United States. With only Mr. Justice Harlan dissenting, that Court upheld Carrington's claim and ordered his admission to the franchise in El Paso.

The opinion of the Court, by Mr. Justice Stewart, puts this decision squarely and solely on the equal

[6] Texas Constitution, Article VI, Section 2.

protection clause of the Fourteenth Amendment. Inevitably, the opinion concedes the general power of the states to set qualifications for voting. This concession made, the inquiry had to be whether the particular limitation imposed was "reasonable." "Reasonable," in this constitutional sense, is a term, normally, of wide latitude; a classification is "reasonable" if a reasonable man might think it advisable, even though other reasonable men might disagree. The state of Texas put forward justifications which I for one find it impossible to classify as wholly capricious and arbitrary, or as "unreasonable" in this constitutional sense. Military personnel, said the state, are subject to special pressures and might be present in such numbers as simply to take over small communities. They come under orders, and they leave when ordered away; their residence is not a matter of their own desire or intention but of military exigence. Mr. Justice Harlan made something like these points in his dissent, and I think he was right.

Yet I agree with the decision in the case on grounds which may illustrate my theme for these lectures—on grounds, moreover, whose entire omission by both Court and counsel illustrates an interesting point about our American juristic style. Carrington, I should rather have said, was a federal soldier, recruited by the national government to perform a crucial national

function. Conceding that in every other way he quali-
fied to vote, Texas said that, solely upon the showing
that he was in the performance of that function, he
was not to vote. It makes little difference whether you
call that a penalization of membership in the national
Army. It is, in neutral terminology, the imposition,
by a state, of a distinctive disadvantage based solely
on membership in the Army. My thought would be
that it ought to be held that no state may annex any
disadvantage simply and solely to the performance of
a federal duty.

Now the stylistic, or, if you like, methodological difference between the reason I would have
given and the reason the Court gave goes to the
essence of what I have to say. The Court (and counsel in the briefs) exhibited our standard preference
for the ground that purports to proceed from interpretation of a particular text. The ground I would
have preferred is one sounding in the structure of
federal union, and in the relation of federal to state
governments; it can point to no particular text as its
authority. This is a mode of reasoning which tends
to be rejected, or ignored as a possibility, by our legal
culture.

I think it is very simple to show, however, that the
logic of national structure, as distinguished from the
topic of particular textual exegesis, has broad validity.

One can do this with extreme cases. Suppose there were no Fourteenth Amendment. Could a state make it a crime to file suit in a federal court? Could a state provide that lifelong disqualification from voting or holding property was to result from even a short service in the United States Army? Could a state prohibit marriage by federal officials, so long as they remained in office? Could a state disqualify voters who would not take an oath to vote for the Republican candidate for Congress? As matters stand, we would prefer, I think, to point to texts, mostly in the Fourteenth Amendment, to establish the unconstitutionality of such extreme actions. But is it not clear that, if those texts were not there, we would point to other texts, so long as we adhered to the textual style? And is it not, further, clear that our real reasons would not be textual, and that if we had no text which by any stretch of its interpreter's will could apply, we would still decide these, and a host of other similarly extreme cases, in the same way, on the substantial ground that such state measures interfere with and impede relations which the national government has set up for its own purposes?

Now you may say these are indeed extreme cases, to the point of cartooning. But every legal method starts with such cases. One of the questions I would raise is why, as amongst different legal methods, equally available, we elect to pursue the textual method from the cartoon case on into the fine grain of real problems while leaving virtually unused the method of inference from political structure. The ground of my objection is well illustrated by *Carrington* v. *Rash*; it is simply that the textual method, in some cases, forces us to blur the focus and talk evasively, while the structural method frees us to talk sense. The action of Texas was not really "arbitrary" in that case; there *are* differences between military people and other people with respect to the meaning of their residence. Giving effect to those differences is well within the latitude we ordinarily allow to the state, in the general case, under the equal protection clause. The real question is whether we think Texas, reasonably or not, should be allowed to annex a disability solely to federal military service.

Early along in every course in constitutional law, one takes up the case of *McCulloch* v. *Maryland*.[7] The great opinion of Mr. Chief Justice Marshall in that case addresses itself to two questions. First, there was the question whether the Congress might permissibly create a corporation to be called and to function as the Bank of the United States. It will be familiar learning to nearly all here that the strong preference of our legal culture for the holding based on the

[7] 4 Wheaton 316 (1819).

specific text is shown by the fact that later comment on the opinion has sometimes treated this part of it as though it rested solidly on the so-called "necessary and proper" clause. A reasonably careful reading shows that Marshall does not place principal reliance on this clause as a ground of decision; that before he reaches it he has already decided, on the basis of far more general implications, that Congress possesses the power, not expressly named, of establishing a bank and chartering corporations; that he addresses himself to the necessary and proper clause only in response to counsel's arguing its *restrictive* force; and that he never really commits himself to the proposition that the necessary and proper clause enlarges governmental power, but only to the propositions, first, that it does not restrict it, and, secondly, that it *may* have been inserted to remove doubt on questions of power which the rest of Article I, Section 8, without the necessary and proper clause, had not, in Marshall's view, really left doubtful.

The second question in the case was whether a state might tax the functioning of the Bank of the United States, admitting the latter to be a validly created national instrumentality. Here I find my students, each year, become rather puzzled. As laymen they have absorbed the layman's notions about constitutional law, and they think it consists, indeed that it must consist, in the interpretation of the commands embodied in particular texts. Yet Marshall's reasoning, on this branch of the case is, as I read it, essentially structural. It has to do in great part with what he conceives to be the warranted relational proprieties between the national government and the government of the states, with the structural corollaries of national supremacy—and, at one point, of the mode of formation of the Union. You can root the result, if you want to (and Marshall sometimes may seem to be doing this) in the supremacy clause of Article VI, but that seems not a very satisfying rationale, for Article VI declares the supremacy of whatever the national law may turn out to be, and does not purport to give content to that law. In this, perhaps the greatest of our constitutional cases, judgment is reached not fundamentally on the basis of that kind of textual exegesis which we tend to regard as normal, but on the basis of reasoning from the total structure which the text has created.

Let us pass down to *Crandall* v. *Nevada*, an entirely unambiguous illustration.[8] That case was decided in 1868. Nevada imposed a tax of a dollar a head on the exit of persons from the state. The opinion of the Court is of the highest methodological interest. There was not yet a Fourteenth Amendment. Counsel sim-

[8] 6 Wallace 35 (1868).

ply assumed that the decision had to go on the interpretation either of the exports-imports clause or of the commerce clause. Mr. Justice Miller, speaking for seven members of the court, said of the posture in which counsel thus left the case: "But we do not concede that the question before us is to be determined by the two clauses of the Constitution which we have been examining."

He goes on to develop a theory of membership in the national polity which includes the right to travel unimpeded from state to state. His support for this theory is relational in a rather elementary sense. He points to the requirements of the national government that its people travel, and to their correlative right to travel to the places at which the national government maintains its offices.

McCulloch v. *Maryland* is cited; it is the emphatic perception of the *Crandall* Court that the *McCulloch* reasoning was structural rather than purely textual.

In a concurrence in the judgment, Mr. Justice Clifford, joined by Chief Justice Chase, stepped back to what at least purportedly was textual ground. Said he:

I agree that the State law in question is unconstitutional and void, but I am not able to concur in the principal reasons assigned in the opinion of the court in support of that conclusion. On the contrary, I hold that the act of the State legislature is inconsistent with the power conferred upon Congress to regulate commerce among the several States, and I think the judgment of the court should have been placed exclusively upon that ground.

This short concurrence marks the modern mode, and indeed the mode of choice in our legal style. The 1941 decision in *Edwards* v. *California* confirms this.[9] Edwards, arguably a "pauper," had been brought into California by his brother-in-law, in violation of a state law prohibiting the introduction of indigent persons. By now there was a Fourteenth Amendment, and everybody had a text. Four Justices chose the "privileges and immunities" clause, citing *Crandall* v. *Nevada*. But the majority of five invalidated the statute on commerce clause grounds.

So far I have mentioned only cases in which state laws might be questioned on the ground of their interfering either with the operation of the federal government or with the direct relations of the individual with that government. Somewhat more roundness can be given to the picture by taking up the case of *Brewer* v. *Hoxie School District No. 46.*[10] The action was brought by the school board against a group of private citizens. The charge was that these people were harassing the school board in an attempt

[9] 314 U.S. 160 (1941).
[10] 238 Federal Reporter, 2d Series, 91 (Eighth Circuit U.S. Court of Appeals, 1956).

to prevent it from fulfilling its own federally created duty to take steps toward desegregating its schools.

Now there is no constitutional text to which, even as a formal matter, one can point and say, "That is the text which makes unlawful, and therefore enjoinable, what these people have done." The plaintiffs cited the supremacy clause, and another clause in Article VI, requiring them, as a school board, to take an oath to support the federal Constitution. But the supremacy clause is of even less specific applicability, if that is possible, than it was in *McCulloch* v. *Maryland*. And the clause requiring state officials to swear loyalty to the federal Constitution defines rather the duty of the plaintiffs than the duty of private individuals not to harass them. The actual reasoning of the court is most interesting:

Plaintiffs are under a duty to obey the Constitution. Const. Art. VI, cl. 2. They are bound by oath or affirmation to support it and are mindful of their obligation. It follows as a necessary corollary that they have a federal right to be free from direct and deliberate interference with the performance of the constitutionally imposed duty. The right arises by necessary implication from the imposition of the duty as clearly as though it had been specifically stated in the Constitution.

The Court then cited a number of cases, in which a purely relational right had been given effect, and decided (rightly, I should think, beyond serious doubt) that the defendants' harassment of the plaintiffs was unlawful as a matter of federal law.

I believe the stylistic preference I have been talking about can be illustrated in another most significant and curiously convoluted way, out of a decisional line among the most important the Supreme Court has marked out. I am referring to the decisions, beginning perhaps with the *Passenger Cases*,[11] and certainly by *Cooley* v. *The Board of Wardens*,[12] in which the Court, finding a negative implication in the commerce clause, has excluded the states from certain regulatory and taxing activity with respect to interstate commerce.

This negative inference, in later years so productive of decision, had a curious early history. Summarily, in *Gibbons* v. *Ogden*, in 1824, the Court stated the contention in one of its forms, but did not choose it for reliance.[13] Then in *Wilson* v. *Blackbird Creek Marsh Co.* (1829), it seemed to be rejecting the notion that the commerce clause contained any implication excluding the states from regulatory activity, in the absence of exercise of the commerce power by Congress.[14] This view, generally speaking, prevailed in

11 7 Howard 283 (1849).
12 12 Howard 299 (1851).
13 9 Wheaton 1 (1824).
14 2 Peters 245 (1829).

New York v. *Miln*,[15] and it was not until 1849, in the *Passenger Cases*, some sixty years after the Constitution went into effect, that the first case was decided in which some of the majority held a state regulation invalid for its supposed repugnancy to the commerce clause. Two years later, in 1851, in *Cooley* v. *The Board of Wardens*, though upholding the particular state law at bar, the Court began to give this subject its modern shape, by saying that some state regulations affecting interstate and foreign commerce would be valid, and some would not be valid, depending on whether or not uniformity of regulation was required by the subject matter. It was not, however, until after the Civil War that this negative inference from the commercial clause, sometimes now presented as so vital to the health of the infant Republic, was at all developed.

If I were not a lover of mercy, I could have prepared myself to spend all three of these lectures discoursing on the variant theories of the various Justices in *New York* v. *Miln* and the *Passenger Cases* alone. I did not do so. I will, however, assert summarily that what sense the subject has finally received—and that is not total sense—has come precisely from its transmutation from a problem in textual construction and single-text implication into a problem about the eco-

[15] 11 Peters 102 (1837).

nomic structure of nationhood—about the implications of the fact that we are one people, commercially as otherwise. It seems to me the textual inference never was a very good one, and certainly it was not one which in any decisive way can be shown to have commended itself in early times. The sense of the matter seems to come from a concept of economic interdependence which is not so much implied logically or legally in the commerce clause as it is evidenced by that clause as well as by other things, including even the Preamble. I do not know how much practical harm was done by the failure to develop such a structural theory at an early time. I am pretty sure that all that is good (in the cases) about the commerce clause negative inference would have been attained if the Court has said forthrightly in the very beginning: "We are, in commerce, a single nation. That nationhood imposes important disabilities on the states. They may do whatever is consonant with it, but may not regulate or tax in any way which jars with it." Such a placing of the matter squarely on grounds of political structure would create enormous problems when one tried to make it more precise, but what "test" purporting to rely on the commerce clause as text, and on an inference from it which is certainly formally invalid, has ever produced problems of less difficulty? On the other hand, the openly structural "one-people" mode of thought might have short-circuited much difficulty, above all by making it instantly quite clear what had to be talked about, without metaphysical complications, if one would justify a result at the concrete level.

I am inclined to think well of the method of reasoning from structure and relation. I think well of it, above all, because to succeed it has to make sense—current, practical sense. The textual-explication method, operating on general language, may often—perhaps more often than not—be made to make sense, by legitimate enough devices of interpretation. But it contains within itself no guarantee that it will make sense, for a court may always present itself or even see itself as being bound by the stated intent, however nonsensical, of somebody else. In *Hoxie School District*, on the other hand, the only way to justify the result was to argue that it was implied, in the nature of the federal-state relationship, that people were forbidden to interfere with state officials who were trying to implement federal rights. I think this an eminently sensible implication. You may not think so. If you do not, then we can and must begin to argue at once about the practicalities and proprieties of the thing, without getting out dictionaries whose entries will not really respond to the question we are putting, or scanning utterances, contemporary with the text, of persons who did not really face the question we are asking. We will have to deal with policy and not with grammar. I am not suggesting that grammar can be sidestepped, or that policy can legitimately be the whole of law. I am only saying that where a fairly available method of legal reasoning, by its very nature, leads directly to the discussion of practical rightness, that method should be used whenever possible. It is the best wisdom of every system of law to seek and to cleave unto such intellectual modes.

How might our federal constitutional law use the method of reasoning from structure and relation? What relations and structures are soundly enough established to furnish a basis for this kind of legal thought? Some possibilities (in part, as we have seen, actualized in practice) suggest themselves.

First, there is the national government itself, as a functioning structure and as a party to relations. *McCulloch* v. *Maryland* started and well illustrates the kind of thought to which this leads, but the development on the whole has been rather meager. If lawyers were trained to think constantly of this heading as a live and productive one, it is my view that such an opinion as the Court uttered in *Carrington* v. *Rash* would never have been written; instead, it would have been held—probably *per curiam* by the Supreme Court of Texas—that the subjecting of a federal soldier, strictly as such and on no other showing than that of his being a federal soldier, to an adverse discrimination, so clearly tended to impede the operation of the national government as to be forbidden quite without regard to its violation of any specific textual guarantee. We would have been spared what I cannot help regarding as an unsound opinion, supporting a sound—indeed something like a necessary—holding.

I think at this point it might be well to mention that there seems to be neither a textual nor a conceptual basis for the importation of any "state action" doctrine into this line of reasoning. The celebrated *Debs* case, as you will recall, upheld the issuance of an injunction against railroad strikers, on the ground, in part, that their actions were obstructing the mails.[16] The political background of the *Debs* case was unpleasant. The obstruction of the mails may not have existed in fact. Under all the circumstances, the Attorney General's (that is to say, the President's) decision to seek an injunction may have been unwise, and such a decision is always a discretionary one. But I think these factors ought not to obscure the soundness of the holding as a matter of law. The very existence and authorized functioning of a national government ought in general to imply the unlawfulness of interference with its performance of those functions,

[16] *In re Debs*, 158 U.S. 564 (1895).

whether or not the interference is performed by a state government.

The concept of interference with national governmental function shades off into the concept of interference with rights created and protected by the national government. These concepts are bound together by the fact that the creation and protection of individual rights is the highest function of any government. Even the carriage of the mails moves toward delivery of the letter as its final cause, and therefore toward the right to receive it. The *Hoxie School District* case makes the point as to "state action." In that case, the action complained of was "private," in the technical sense. It is true that the school board plaintiff was a state agency, but it was very far from denying anybody equal protection of the laws. "No state," to quote the phrase which has given verbal underpinning to the state action doctrine, was doing anything in violation of a constitutional guarantee. Private individuals, acting on their own, were trying to coerce an agency of the state not to comply with the Constitution. I cannot see why it makes any difference whether this private action was aimed at a school board or at a private person resting under some federal obligation. Let us take the case of a restaurant owner who wants and tries to comply with the Civil Rights Act of 1964, by receiving Negroes freely in his restaurant, but who is threatened with or subjected to physical, social, or economic coercion by those who want him to violate the act by keeping his restaurant white. It is true that the restaurant owner, unlike the school board, has not taken an Article VI oath to support the Constitution. But he, no whit less than they, is under a definite obligation to obey national law. I can see no reason why, if a federal court may enjoin interference with their obedience, a federal court may not enjoin interference with his obedience. And there is in the one case no more reason than in the other to ask whether the action interfering with obedience is "state action" or "private action." The unhallowed "state action" doctrine takes its origin from operations performed, in the *Civil Rights Cases* of 1883, on particular texts; where the right at stake is not derived from those or any similar texts, the doctrine itself has no right to live.[17]

Let me develop this idea in another direction by mentioning its aptness to dissolve many doubts as to congressional power, or at least to enable these to be placed on a basis, more closely adapted morally to the evils than is the commerce clause. It is hard nowadays to remember, for example, what the objections were to a federal anti-lynching bill. The sheriff who holds a prisoner holds him subject to a federally sanctioned

[17] 109 U.S. 3 (1883)

rule that he shall not be deprived of life or liberty without due process of law. To take him out of the sheriff's custody for the purpose of frustrating the performance of this federal obligation would seem to me a federal wrong in strict analogy to the one enjoined in the Hoxie School District case. But even if you cannot go that far with me, how can it be thought that Congress may not prevent, by penalizing it, this kind of interference with processes commanded by federal law?

I will mention today only one other great heading under which I would classify those relations which seem to me to furnish ground for problem-solving inferences. I am referring to the concept of nationhood which I take to underlie *Crandall* v. *Nevada*. That opinion took its stand on rather narrow ground. It based the holding on a reciprocal relation between the national government which might have need for its citizens to travel, and their right to travel. I should think, first, that on the face of things the *Crandall* rationale cannot be limited to *citizens*. The national governmental requirements for mobility which it states apply quite as much to non-citizens as to citizens; they apply on their face to all the people in the United States. But I think the ground of *Crandall* v. *Nevada* ought to be more radically restated. By 1868 —and if not by then, then certainly by 1968—the fact that the United States is a single nation warrants inference as to mobility of population, quite aside from strictly governmental needs. It is hard to doubt that this is really behind the decision in *Edwards* v. *California*, though the Court chooses to rest that decision on the commerce clause. As we have seen, that clause, wherever it is sensibly applied as a ground for nullifying state laws, functions transparently as a mere parameter connecting the particular problem with the concept of nationhood—in most cases economic nationhood, but in *Edwards* nationhood of people. The majority in *Edwards* may have rejected the "privileges and immunities" ground because, as the text of the Fourteenth Amendment would have it, that ground is linked to citizenship. But if the parameter be altogether short-circuited, and we feel that the time has come when we can openly talk of the right to travel within the country as an inference from national unity, then there is no reason why such an inference should not protect the right of the lawfully resident alien quite as much as it protects that of the citizen.

At the very least, I am expressing here an aesthetic and moral preference, though aesthetic and moral choices may have their effects, ultimately, in practice as well. I should prefer to think of Edwards' right to travel, and of his brother-in-law's right to bring him into the state, as a consequence of his being one of the people in a unitary nation, to which, because of its nationhood, internal barriers to travel are unthinkable, rather than pretending that I have performed a warranted inference from a clause empowering Congress to regulate commerce among the several states. I am pretty sure that it was the first of these thoughts, rather than the second, that really moved the Court in the *Edwards* case; indeed, this is the next thing to express in the opinions, both in that of the five judges who employed the commerce clause theory, and in that of the four who employed the privileges and immunities clause. Why should one not explicitly base such holdings, not on Humpty-Dumpty textual manipulation, but on the sort of political inference which not only underlies the textual manipulation but is, in a well constructed opinion, usually invoked to support the interpretation of the cryptic text?

Let me finish, for tonight, with two points. The first is that, in suggesting the possibility of a wider use of inference from relation and structure in the intellectual processes of constitutional law, I do not think I am suggesting that precision be supplanted by wide-open speculation. The precision of textual explication is nothing but specious in the areas that matter. Mr. Maurice Merrill has recently movingly pled for fidelity to the constitutional text.[18] His plea has some good things in it. But he seems to me to weigh insufficiently the real problems of good faith divergence in interpretation. He regards the case of *Shelley* v. *Kraemer*, for example, as a clear case of lack of respect for the text, presumably because of the "No state shall" language of the equal protection clause under which that case was decided.[19] But that phrase merely sets, rather than solves, the problem whether a state which provides a recordation machinery for racial restrictive covenants, functionally similar to racial zoning, and then enforces them by injunctive process in its courts, is "denying equal protection" to the disfavored race. A host of respectable commentators have disagreed with him. He, on the other hand, would be content with a Thirteenth Amendment theory for the case, a theory which to some will seem to involve at least as great verbal difficulties. The question is not whether the text shall be respected, but rather how one goes about respecting a text of that high generality and consequent ambiguity which marks so many crucial constitutional texts. I submit that the generalities and ambiguities are no greater when one applies the method

[18] *Constitutional Interpretation: The Obligation to Respect the Text*, in PERSPECTIVES OF LAW, ESSAYS FOR AUSTIN WAKEMAN SCOTT, p. 260 (1964).

[19] 334 U.S. 1 (1948).

of reasoning from structure and relation. I submit that the opinion in *McCulloch* v. *Maryland* has just as satisfying a legal quality as the opinions in *Fletcher* v. *Peck*[20] and the *Dartmouth College Case*,[21] where the obligation of contracts clause was being interpreted, after the preferred mode of our legal culture.

Finally, I have learned so to fear the maxim *expressio unius* that I must timidly correct a doubtless nonexistent impression that what I have suggested is the total abandonment of the method of particular-text interpretation. It is entirely plain, on the contrary, that so long as we continue to look on our Constitution as a part of the law applicable in court, just so long the work of sheer textual interpretation will be a great part—probably the greatest part—of judicial work in constitutional law. There is, moreover, a close and perpetual interworking between the textual and the relational and structural modes of reasoning, for the structure and relations concerned are themselves created by the text, and inference drawn from them must surely be controlled by the text.

All I am suggesting is that a method not unknown in our constitutional law be brought more clearly into the conscious field of those who work in that law. I

[20] 6 Cranch 87 (1810).
[21] 4 Wheaton 518 (1819).

make this suggestion in the faith, fundamentally, that clarity about what we are doing, about the true or the truly acceptable grounds of judgment, is both a good in itself, and a means to sounder decision.

II · Some Particular Structural Considerations in Constitutional Law

The late Jack Carson once played a role which required him to drink a gin and tonic, while he stood, wrapped in a towel, in a Turkish bath. A companion asked him why he was drinking gin in these unusual surroundings. "I have a cold," he said, "I always use gin for colds." He paused, and smiled wryly. He added: "But then, you know, I use it for everything."

There are fifty-two words which we come close to using for everything. I am referring to the three celebrated prohibitory clauses in the Fourteenth Amendment.

Since the privileges and immunities clause has so far almost never been affirmatively applied, virtually the whole work of shielding the individual from the incidence of state power, in the name of national standards of freedom, equality, and justice, has been done by the due process and equal protection clauses.

Where would we be, I wonder, if it had happened that these three clauses were not there? It is a teasing question. Can it be that all the protection we now trace to these clauses would simply be missing, if the obscure and hectic process by which the Fourteenth Amendment came into being had suffered some kind of deflection, so that the text did not include these fifty-two words—only thirty-one, in fact, if you insulate, as the Court in effect has thus far done, the privileges and immunities clause? If so, then by state law Negroes could be barred from jury service, penalized more severely than whites for the same crimes, and kept from riding the railroads—or, as far as one can tell, even from owning bicycles, or from learning to read. A state could put a man in jail for twenty years for advocating the passage of a state income tax law, or for not attending the services of the state church. State trials for crime could be dominated by mobs, or held before judges whose pay depended upon conviction. State searching and interrogation procedures could be just as oppressive and unfair as the state wanted to make them. The soldier, drafted by the nation to fight in a national war, would come home to find that the nation threw not the most minimum safeguards around him, gave him no protection in return for the sacrifice it had exacted. Is that picture really necessary?

Some modern thought is moving toward the point of view that it is not really necessary—that the prohibitory guarantees of Section I of the Fourteenth Amendment need not have been made to carry the whole weight. Some of the weight, I will suggest here, might have been transferred, or might still be transferred, to the process of inference from status and relationships, these of course in turn created by the Constitution.

What is it that protects the freedom of speech, the freedom of utterance, against infringement by the states? The basic textual guarantee is in the First Amendment, leading off the Bill of Rights. But *Barron* v. *Baltimore*,[1] in 1833, settled the law to the effect that the Bill of Rights does not apply to the action of the states, and the First Amendment certainly would not seem, on its face, to apply to the actions of the states, because it lays its prohibition on Congress by name, and while it seems quite reasonable to extend this to include federal agencies drawing their power from Congress, and of an inferior dignity to Congress's, he would be an intrepid reader who would read it to apply it to the state governments.

Salvation, as all know, came through the "due process" clause of the Fourteenth Amendment. After a couple of stalled starts, the Court in 1925 decided the celebrated *Gitlow* case.[2] Gitlow had published a cloudily worded manifesto, which could perhaps uncharitably be construed as a general call for violent

[1] 7 Peters 243 (1833).
[2] 268 U.S. 652 (1925)

revolution. He had been convicted under the New York criminal anarchy act. It was in this case that the Supreme Court first held that the "liberty" protected in the due process clause of the Fourteenth Amendment included the "freedom of speech and of the press" protected by the First Amendment. It would seem that the particular-text method of constitutional interpretation had come up with a highly satisfactory result.

Yet, as the thing worked out, the result was not altogether satisfactory—not so satisfactory as to make quite idle any inquiry as to whether an alternative theoretical road may not be possible. The first ominous fact was that Gitlow went to jail after all. It is necessary to be very clear on how it was that this could happen, after the Court had just finished announcing that the freedom of speech in the First Amendment was included among the liberties guaranteed by the Fourteenth. It must be remembered that the Fourteenth Amendment does no more than forbid the states to deprive persons of liberty "without due process of law." What is "due process of law," in this context? There was considerable authority, at the time of the *Gitlow* decision, for the proposition that "due process of law" was wanting only when there was no rational connection between the legislation and an objective the legislature might legitimately seek. This standard,

if honestly applied, almost always results in the ratifi-
cation of the judgment of the legislature. And the
Court, in *Gitlow*, faithfully followed this standard.
After pointing out that the legislature might ration-
ally conclude the advocacy of revolution had a tendency to produce substantive evils, the Court in very
clear language summed up the ground for its holding:
"We cannot hold that the present statute is an arbitrary or unreasonable exercise of the police power of
the state, unwarrantably infringing the freedom of
speech or press; and we must and do sustain its constitutionality."

The *Gitlow* case, then, did in a way stretch the protection of the Fourteenth Amendment to include freedom of utterance. But it did so at the price of limiting
the protection to cases of "arbitrary and unreasonable
exercise of the police power of the state." And the legislature, the Court expressly says in the *Gitlow* opinion, is to have the benefit of "every presumption,"
when the statute's "arbitrariness" is being assessed.
The *Gitlow* case did not at all lay on the states a flat
prohibition against their abridging the freedom of
speech. It applied the same rule to state laws infringing the freedom of speech that held good for state
laws in general—they must not be "arbitrary." That is
very little protection for free speech.

Now this is not a necessary consequence of applying the Fourteenth Amendment to free speech cases, for it is possible to read "due process of law" in other ways, and to insist that it sets a higher standard, as to legislation infringing certain interests, than mere abstention from wholly arbitrary action. In effect, this gloss has been put upon the phrase in later cases involving state legislation penalizing utterances. But *Gitlow* was never squarely overruled—has not to this day been squarely overruled—and the thought of *Gitlow*—that state legislation penalizing speech must be "arbitrary" before it violates the national constitution—has continued to exert a sort of influence.

One faintly but balefully visible point of influence is the citation of *Gitlow*, without categorical disapproval, in the celebrated 1951 *Dennis* case, wherein the convictions of Communist leaders were sustained on a federal charge of conspiring to teach the propriety of overthrowing the government.[3] It is not possible to say how much influence the *Gitlow* line of reasoning had on the result in *Dennis*. What one can say, categorically, is that that line of reasoning was radically out of place in, had no relevance to, a case concerning, as *Dennis* did, the application not of the due process clause to a state law, but of the First Amendment to an Act of Congress. What should have been said about *Gitlow* in *Dennis*, if anything was to be

[3] 341 U.S. 494 (1951).

said about it, was that the first case had nothing to do with the second. The fact that that was not said, that the case was cited as in a relevant line, makes one suspect that the *Gitlow* thought may, in this confused field, have had some influence on the First Amendment law of free speech, where concepts such as "due process," "reasonableness," and "arbitrariness" ought never to have played any part. Certainly, the *Dennis* opinion's dilution of the clear and present danger test looks suspiciously like a muddled and disguised form of "due process" reasoning.

These confusions lead the mind to search for a more adequate basis for federal constitutional protection against state interferences with the freedom of speech. It would be my thesis that such a basis exists —that the nature of the federal government, and of the states' relations to it, compels the inference of some federal constitutional protection for free speech, and gives to a wide protection an inferential support quite as strong as the textual support we have been examining. Several years ago, I made this suggestion in a little book on constitutional law;[4] tonight I would like to expand on it.

I have used strong language—I have said that the inference of some federal constitutional protection against state infringement of freedom of utterance is

[4] PERSPECTIVES IN CONSTITUTIONAL LAW, p. 93 (1963).

compelled. Let me start with the matter of petition. The First Amendment says that Congress shall make no law abridging the right of the people peaceably to assemble and to petition the government for a redress of grievances. *Barron* v. *Baltimore*, as we have seen, held that the Bill of Rights, of which this provision is a part, did not apply against the states. But is it not an inference from structure and relation, just as sure as any constitutional inference could be, that no state could constitutionally make criminal the signing and transmittal of any petition to Congress? Is it not perfectly clear that no state could constitutionally do this for some petitions, on the basis of their contents? I would assert that it is. Not because the First Amendment forbids it—the First Amendment, in its clear terms, does not speak to the problem. I should make my assertion rather because such a state law would constitute interference with a transaction which is a part of the working of the federal government. I think that would be true even if there were no First Amendment, for the petitioning of a legislative body would seem to be an inherent part of its relation with its constituency. The state penalization of petitioners on the basis of the contents of their petitions would seem to me like the state penalization of federal court plaintiffs for the content of their complaints—a state's meddling with the vital relations between the national government and its people.

But is it very much less certain that this protection must extend to the stages leading up to petition? The petition provision in the First Amendment is directly linked to a provision concerning peaceable assembly. What certainly is meant is assembly for the discussion of public questions, discussion which might lead to petition. And it seems rather clear that such assembly, like petition itself, is a part of the working of the national government; its conduct and its fruits in opinion are the clearly contemplated material of that government's action, a part of the flow of communication which is its lifeblood.

I have first mentioned petition and assembly because they are recognized by the First Amendment as components in the national governmental process. But the First Amendment is only evidentiary of what would in any case be reasonably obvious—that petition and assembly for the discussion of national governmental measures are rights founded on the very nature of a national government running on public opinion. If I am not mistaken in this, then I can hardly be mistaken in the conclusion that interference with these rights would be forbidden to the states even if the magical fifty-two words had never come out of the Committee of Fifteen in 1866. Let me leave, for the moment, the petition and assembly point, and mention other relations on which, it seems to me, similar inferences might be rested.

The one that leaps to mind is of course the voting and representation system set up in Article I and in the Seventeenth Amendment. I think one may warrantably add, though it is not essential to do so, the Presidential election system which has *de facto* come into being as a quasi-constitutional gloss on Article II. But I will emphasize the congressional field, as one having indubitable warrant.

Again, I make bold to assert, that from the very structure of the relation between the national representative and his constituency, there arises a compelling inference of some national constitutional protection of free utterance, as against state infringement. Is it conceivable that a state, entirely aside from the Fourteenth or for that matter the First Amendment, could permissibly forbid public discussion of the merits of candidates for Congress, or of issues which have been raised in the congressional campaign, or which an inhabitant of the district—or of the state, where the election is senatorial—might wish to see raised in the campaign? I start with that as the hard core, because I cannot see how anyone could think our national government could run, or was by anybody at any time ever expected to run, on any less openness of public communication than that.

But I see no reason here for sticking to this hard core. Representatives are not in communication with their constituencies only at election time. Letters, even open letters to Congressmen, would seem well within the protected area. I would unhesitatingly go further and say that discussion of all questions which are in the broadest sense relevant to Congress's work is, quite strictly, a part of the working of the national government. If it is not, what is our mechanism for accommodating national political action to the needs and desires of the people? And if it is, does it not reasonably follow that a state may not interfere with it?

I think others of our constitutional relations and structures furnish grounds for similar inferences. The initiation and conduct of litigation in the federal courts—or even in the state courts where what is at stake is a federal right which Article VI commands the state judges to effectuate—requires at least some communication; sometimes it requires quite a lot. Is it possible that a state has a right to interfere in this process? State officials have important federal duties, imposed by the Constitution; they are required by Article VI to swear to support the Constitution; the state legislatures play a vital part in the amendment process and in some other less crucially important fed-

eral matters. Can it be that public discussion of anything connected with their fidelity to the Article VI
oath, or with their performance of these other federal
obligations is not a protected phase of discussion of
national matters by the people of the nation?

I cannot tonight trace every one of these lines of
thought to its every implication. I would say two
things. First, if you admit the validity of this form of
inference at all, then I cannot see any ground for hesi-
tation in going along with it a good way. Nobody can
really doubt, for example, when one thinks about the
affirmative powers that Congress has been held to
possess—under the commerce clause, under the taxing
power, under the power to spend for the general wel-
fare—that public discussion and expression of views
over a very wide range of topics—perhaps over the
whole range of political problems—is in fact connected with possible congressional action, soon or late.
There would seem to be no reason for choking off ar-
bitrarily the federal protection for this process of opin-
ion-formation within the federal political process. Secondly, it would seem likely that full development, in
this spirit, of the concept of federal protection for that
expression which does connect with the federal governmental process—petition, election, judicial pro-
ceedings, Presidential action, and so on—would result
in a merging of boundaries, and at last would eventu-

ate in the conclusion that most serious public discussion of political issues is really a part, at least in one aspect, of the process of national government, and hence ought to be invulnerable to state attack—not on First Amendment grounds, not on due process grounds, but on *McCulloch* v. *Maryland*[5] and *Crandall* v. *Nevada* grounds.[6]

Nothing, it may be, is drier than the discussion of alternative grounds for holdings already reached. But I think there remains some interest in the quest for a firmer basis than we have so far elaborated for federal protection against state measures suppressing freedom of utterance. We must remember that a great leap had to be taken, before the Fourteenth Amendment could do any good in this field—the leap from the base-line normal meaning of "due process of law" to a special requirement of justification for state enactments of this sort. This leap, as we have seen, was not taken in *Gitlow*; it came later, and its length was not everywhere measured the same. From time to time some Justices have alluded to the leap with some indication that it might not in their minds be as long a leap as some other Justices, and some of the rest of us, would like to think. I for one can sleep sounder if I do not have to force my conviction that the states are

[5] 4 Wheaton 316 (1819).
[6] 6 Wallace 35 (1868).

barred from interfering with political speech through the narrow verbal funnel of due process of law.

I think, also, that at least the holdings in some modern cases seem firmer in the light of the concept I have been elaborating. Let me take the great case of *New York Times Co.* v. *Sullivan*, decided in 1964.[7] In that case, Sullivan, one of the elected commissioners in Montgomery, Alabama, sued the *Times* for running an advertisement in which his official conduct was, as he alleged, criticized. For the first time, the court was asked to decide whether and to what extent private libel suits raised free speech questions. The Court held for the *Times*, basing its judgment on the ground that the published criticism was of official conduct—thus generally designated—and that "actual malice" had not been shown. Remember that these precise criteria purport, formally, to come into being by interpretation of two constitutional texts in coaction—the text of the First Amendment, laying a prohibition on Congress, and the text of the Fourteenth Amendment, forbidding a state to deprive any person of liberty or property without due process of law. For my part, I should feel that a firmer and more sensible basis had been laid for the holding if the Court had been in a doctrinal position to take as its ground the most conspicuous thing about the facts of the case—

[7] 376 U.S. 254 (1964).

that the advertisement, on the plaintiff's own allegations, was a public criticism of a state official for his alleged infidelity to his obligation to respect and enforce the federal constitutional guarantee of racial equality; the whole incident was nothing but an episode in a struggle of the highest possible national political interest. It seems to me to make sense, right in the area where you need to make sense, to say that no Alabama judge or jury can penalize free expression with respect to matters of such high national political interest. To me as a lawyer, that ground is at least as satisfying as a "due process" ground, and to me as a believer in federalism it explains what business the Supreme Court has in the situation. Such a ground would have left it open to the Court, moreover, as the ground it took does not, to refuse to deal with every judgment for damages which a state official gets against somebody who has accused him of misusing a county automobile.

It seems to me, similarly, that the opinion in *NAACP v. Button*, decided in 1963, again plays Hamlet with only oblique reference to the Prince of Denmark—by which I mean the substantial national political interest which was being infringed.[8] Virginia had passed a statute both enlarging and making more specific certain ancient rules about the solicitation of

[8] 371 U.S. 415 (1963).

legal business and the conduct of litigation. Rather transparently, the law was for the purpose of harassing the NAACP, and a divided Court judged it unconstitutional. I will not attempt to summarize the Court's Fourteenth Amendment grounds in this case; I will only say that for me the Court would have been on firmer ground, because it would have been talking about what was really at stake, if it could simply have said that the activities of the NAACP under attack were of the highest federal political and legal interest, being wholly aimed at litigation in the federal courts, or in the state courts under the supremacy clause, in furtherance of vital nationally created rights—and that, quite aside from the Fourteenth Amendment, no state had any business interfering in a process so crucially concerned with the implementation of national rights.

When one proposes a new theoretical approach to a problem, one must face the fact that one's hearers are likely to feel somewhat at sea, and to object that the new line of reasoning will lead too far, or that its general formulas afford no ground for prediction of results. To this I would first reply that this theory of protection against state infringements needs to lead no further than the point where a legitimate national political interest is no longer fairly discernible; opinions will differ on that, but at least they would be differing on exactly the right thing, and that is no small gain in law. Secondly, I should reply that there is no loss whatever in certainty, as against the actually prevalent mode. That mode has to begin, as we have seen, with the decision, taken on grounds altogether extrinsic to the text or to anything that could be called interpretation of it, that "due process of law" states a different standard in the free speech case from the one it states in the case involving economic regulation. But even after that is accomplished, fine-grain decisions have to be made, such as the ones made in the *New York Times* case; it is idle to pretend that the text really dictates these decisions, or even helps in arriving at them. Nothing but a possible gain in predictability could come from selection of a ground which forces one to talk about, and only about, realistic factors of national political involvement.

One great change might ensue if the Court could ever be induced to accept this relational argument. It contains no built-in "state action" requirement. Let us go back to the case of *Collins* v. *Hardyman,* decided in 1951.[9] Essentially, the defendants in that case were charged with breaking up a public meeting held for the discussion of national public issues. The Court upheld a dismissal of the complaint, on the ground that the applicable Act of Congress did not cover the ac-

[9] 341 U.S. 651 (1951).

tions of private individuals. I would only say now that I think a fuller insight into the nature of such discussion as a part of the national political process might force a reconsideration of the result in the case, and certainly ought to wipe out any doubt as to the constitutional power of Congress to make criminal any violent interference, whether by a state or by private persons, with the opinion-forming process that gives life to the national polity.

Finally, on this whole matter, let me say that I do not believe I have once used the word "citizen." I am not proposing a broad interpretation of the privileges and immunities clause of the Fourteenth Amendment, which protects only citizens. I am proposing a mode of inference, from the political relations which bind all the people who are a part of the intercommunicating polity that is the United States. This polity, I should think it plain, comprises all the people lawfully here, including, of course, those aliens whom Congress has deliberately seen fit to receive among us. Their desires and discontents, their thoughts and feelings, are and always traditionally have been a part of the material out of which our politics constitutes itself.

I do not want to leave this subject without acknowledging my obvious debt to the late Professor

Alexander Meiklejohn.[10] He above others has made us perceive the political framework in which the free speech guarantee makes sense. I differ from him, however, at least as I understand him, in that I am not here putting these political considerations forward as helps in the interpretation of the First Amendment, but rather as independent structural grounds supporting the inference of federal protection of free speech against the actions of the states. I ought to add that of course nothing I have said has the slightest tendency to suggest diminishment of the force of the First Amendment, and I fully agree with Professor Meiklejohn that that amendment ought to be held to bar all congressional interference with political speech.

I intend to use the rest of my time tonight to mention and open up—in a way even more preliminary and tentative than has been the case with the one example I have so far discussed—a few more fields in which, as it seems to me, results quite similar to those which have been achieved under the fifty-two words we are imagining to be excised from the Fourteenth Amendment might conceivably have been achieved by reasonings from the relations in which we stand to our governments. I use the plural advisedly, for I intend here to deal with *citizenship*, with state as well as fed-

[10] FREE SPEECH AND ITS RELATION TO SELF-GOVERNMENT (1948).

eral citizenship, since the very first clause of the Fourteenth Amendment—one we are not blotting out in imagination—makes it a national rule that every person born in the country or naturalized shall be a citizen both of the nation and of his state. This clause has recently received a vitalizing interpretation in *Afroyim* v. *Rusk*,[11] where it was held that this citizenship is indelible except by the voluntary act of the individual—a holding which seems to me to firm up in a most desirable way the solemn dignity of our citizenship, without diminishing to any significant extent the power of government to deal, by the normal mechanisms of trial and punishment, with any actions that ought to be punished—without, indeed, taking away from government the power to withdraw diplomatic protection from citizens abroad who either are acting in serious ways against the national interest, but who cannot be laid hold of, or who in some unmistakable way show their lack of continuing attachment to the United States. But I am concerned tonight with the internal implications of the national declaration of state and national citizenship.

I must also say that I use the word "citizen" hesitatingly. In the end, I think it will be possible to show that, for a separate reason, inference of rights from citizenship need not put the lawfully resident alien

[11] 387 U.S. 253 (1967).

at any serious disadvantage. But I will return to this point later.

No sensible discussion of the citizenship relation, as created or confirmed by the Fourteenth Amendment, can start anywhere but with the Negro, for it is clear beyond peradventure that the prime and dominating purpose of this part of the Fourteenth Amendment was to do something about the status of the Negro. Even if this were not so, the primacy of the race problem would subsist for another reason—for the contemporary reason that our citizenship is sick with the disease of racism; if "citizenship" even poetically, even as a word of exhortation, has something to do with incorporation and participation in society, then it is here that the trouble is sorest. It will be my submission that attention to the citizenship relation might substantially help in healing what needs to be healed.

I have to say that herein I am walking over recent footsteps—those of Professor Arthur Kinoy, whose article,[12] published last fall, stated the case in considerable analytic and historical depth for our revitalizing the elder Justice Harlan's views in dissent in the *Civil Rights Cases* of 1883, and finding in the command that the Negro shall be a citizen a command not merely that he rejoice in that honorific label, but also

[12] *The Constitutional Right of Negro Freedom*, 21 Rutgers Law Review 387 (1967).

that he be allowed, both by the state and by those
who actually control the matter, to participate fully
in the public life of the society of which he is a citizen.[13] I shall not try to improve either on Justice Harlan or on Professor Kinoy, but will add a few periph-
eral observations.

Why, at this late date, should we be looking about
for another theory of Negro rights? It is the equal protection clause on which principal—indeed virtually
exclusive—reliance has so far been placed, so far as
judicial activity is concerned. And both judicial and
congressional activity have been thought permissible,
under the equal protection clause, only when the dis-
criminatory practice from which the Negro suffers is
the result of "state action." I have recently had occasion to work over the "state action" doctrine, accept-
ing the issues it raises in their own terms, and my conclusion, like that of many other writers, has been
that there is not much in it any more.[14] "State action"
is not very hard to find in the usual racial equal protection case, unless you have rather firmly decided
in advance that you are going to make it hard to find,
by setting up special criteria which have no warrant
in the language of the equal protection clause or in

[13] 109 U.S. 3 (1883).
[14] Black, *Foreword: "State Action," Equal Protection, and
California's Proposition 14,* in *The Supreme Court, 1966
Term,* 81 Harvard Law Review 69 (1967).

the cases. But it would be handy, and relieving, to find an alternative to the recurrent search of each record for those state involvements which, it seems, always turn out to be there, but which often fall into some new pattern, so that, while there is no precedent against you, there is none with you foursquare. Such an alternative may exist in the citizenship relation.

When it comes to congressional action, Congress has been reluctant to take a flexible and realistic view on "state action," and has therefore based some of its most important measures in this field on the commerce power. Now I do not think there is anything affirmatively wrong in this. The commerce power seems to me rightly invoked, for example, in Title II of the Civil Rights Act of 1964, commanding service without discrimination by all establishments serving or offering to serve interstate travelers, or getting a substantial part of their supplies in interstate commerce.[15] As to the first criterion, the terms and conditions on which interstate travelers are served when they stop seem to me just as much a part of the manner in which interstate commerce is conducted as are the conditions of service in a railroad dining car. It is a trivial difference that one establishment is itself on wheels, while the other is where the wheels bring the traveler. Beyond that, the question is just

[15] 78 United States Statutes at Large 241.

how great an evil you think racial discrimination is, and how far you consequently are willing to go to eliminate it from interstate travel. If, as I do, you think it a very great evil, the dominating evil of our national life, then you really want to see that it never happens that an interstate traveler is inconvenienced or humiliated because of his race, and the only way to bring that about is to prohibit racial discrimination wherever even one such traveler might stop and be refused service. In fact, this means all public restaurants; it is fact and not fiction that once in a while any restaurant open to the public will attract an interstate traveler. And since it is utterly impractical to go into the question of his indentification as such, in fact and in law, on the spot, the only way to be sure he will not be discriminated against on racial grounds is to forbid racial discrimination altogether in all restaurants which, by offering to serve the public, inevitably are offering to serve interstate travelers. This, as I say, is an unimpeachable chain of reasoning factually, and whether you want to follow it out to its end is a function not of its factual validity but of your own assessment of the seriousness of the evil. Similarly, if you think racial discrimination is as bad as child labor, then you will not want interstate commerce to supply those who practice it, any more than you want the interstate economy to support child labor by including the shipment of goods made by child labor. Whether you prohibit the shipment to the discriminating establishment, or discrimination by the receiver of the interstate shipment, is a mere question of convenience in enforcement of your rule that shipment of goods in interstate commerce is not to contribute substantially to the practice of racial discrimination.

But, while I believe in the soundness of this reasoning, I can express my objection to Congress's heavy reliance on this ground by saying that I think it is rather poor rhetoric. Too many people, not reading Title II with care, for example, seem to think that Congress has relied on some assessment of remote and doubtful "effects" of discrimination on the flow of commerce; Congress really relied on its power to regulate directly the conditions under which interstate travel is performed, and on its power to prohibit interstate trade serving the specific end of discrimination, and not at all on any remote calculations of general economic effect. But the misunderstanding persists. I think the rhetoric is poor in a deeper sense, even for those who understand the logic. There remains a certain indirection, an inaptness of the logic to cover the whole result. The result of the "offer to serve interstate travelers" criterion, if the act is obeyed and enforced, is that no racial discrimination at all is possible in public restaurants, whether or not the individual discriminee is an interstate traveler. This is not a bad result, and Congress cannot be asked to refrain from exerting its powers to the absolute limit merely because good results, outside the scope of the power invoked, will inevitably ensue. But the discrepancy between justification and result remains, requiring constant explanation, and suggesting, though in my view erroneously, possible disingenuousness. As to the other criterion, the receipt by the discriminating establishment of goods shipped in interstate commerce, Congress is invoking its power over things to bring about results in the lives of men; there is plenty of precedent for this, but there hangs about all of these uses a feeling that the tool employed, though its use was licit and it did the job, was not the perfectly adapted tool.

I would wish, therefore, that Congress, if it passes, let us say, a comprehensive open housing statute, might include in the preamble of such an act both an invocation of its power to redress and supply the want of sufficient state protection, under the equal protection clause, and, under the citizenship clause, its power to declare and give effect to the rights of citizenship as positive rights to full membership in the community, without segregation and isolation. Such declarations would put Congress on record as giving full and affirmative meaning to every part of Section 1 of the Fourteenth Amendment, as repudiating at last the needlessly austere reading of that section which we inherit from a past that thoroughly disliked the ideas of equality and of full citizenship for the Negro. The country would be given, in such a preamble, the true and profoundly noncommercial reasons for the action taken. And I have no doubt not only that the court would uphold legislation resting on this basis, but would follow Congress's lead and abandon the searching of each record for the element of "state action," relying instead, in its judicial work, on the theories Congress would have enunciated.

The relation of citizenship seems to me to embody a sound and healthy rhetoric for two other connected reasons. First, our use of this concept in the work of law could be the beginning of an answer to the growing separatism of the Black Power movement, for it would sum up in a word the thing we ought to be offering in place of that withdrawal to which many Negroes—in my view, naturally though regrettably—feel themselves driven. Its effectiveness in this regard would altogether depend on the honesty of the offer, and I do not think for a moment that the white population, North or South, is yet honestly making any bona fide offer of fellow-citizenship, but the substitution of the concept of citizenship for the concept, for example, of the regulation of interstate commerce might at least mark a start toward a view of our relations which men of both races ought to try to reach. On the other hand, I think the concept of citizenship might be a useful corrective to another concept—that of "brotherhood"—which played so prominent a part a few years ago in the utterances of the opponents of racism. I have to say that it seems to me that this word embodied a concept deeply wrong. It suggested that the public demand was that some men had a duty to feel toward and to treat other men as brothers. This, I submit, is an over-reaching, a basic defect in theory, a radically wrong symbolism. That demand never can be made as of right; to make it invites disappointment, and may easily tend to frighten and repel those on whom the demand is made. Brotherly love may stand somewhere in the shadow of time, waiting. There is not very much that law can do about that. But fellow-citizenship is for now, for the day before yesterday. The robust clarity, the received authority of right law, could make no greater symbolic contribution to the theory of our race relations than by using this concept as its chief building material.

As to this part of my lecture tonight, I am very much aware of the fact that I have not talked law directly. I have rather given reasons why law ought to take a long second look at the concept of citizenship, in its bearing on racism, put forward by Mr. Justice Harlan the elder and recently restated by Professor Kinoy. I shall have much the same purpose in the two other brief things I have to say, about the bearings of the citizenship relation on the problem of religious freedom, and the problem of the administration of criminal justice.

I have been reading lately the interesting article of the late Professor Mark De Wolfe Howe on the problem of religious freedom.[16] His views are those of a moderate, with respect to the scope of federal constitutional inhibitions on state dealings with religion. He addresses himself very explicitly to the problem—quite similar to the *Gitlow* problem I have discussed this evening—of the so-called "incorporation" of the First Amendment's religious guarantees by the Fourteenth Amendment. His conclusion is that the Fourteenth Amendment incorporates as much of the First Amendment as protects freedom from anything like religious coercion, from any state invasion of the individual's religious independence, since such invasions violate what he calls, in a phrase well known from Supreme Court opinions, "the

[16] *Religion and The Free Society: The Constitutional Question*, in SELECTED ESSAYS ON CONSTITUTIONAL LAW (Ed. Barrett and others, 1963) p. 780.

scheme of ordered liberty." He thinks, however, that the Fourteenth Amendment does not lay on the states a federal constitutional prohibition against aids to religion which do not invade anyone's freedom—aids such as the furnishing of textbooks to parochial school children, or bussing them to and from school. Unless you give me another year to prepare, and another three lectures in which to do it, I am not going to go into the troubled questions of state aid to religion. But I would point out that a rule such as the one Professor Howe has recommended could seemingly be derived quite as well from the relations of citizenship as from the phrase "due process of law." The use of the concept of "ordered liberty" as a parameter seems to me to make this clear. Can it be that the man who is positively declared to be a citizen of the United States and of the state wherein he resides does not enjoy, by virtue of standing in that relationship, the right to live under a "scheme of ordered liberty"? That would seem to be the least possible domestic implication of the conferral of citizenship, unless one is prepared to say that all that relationship implies is the privilege of writing "citizen" after your name. If the due process clause only gets us, in some fields of its application, as far as a "scheme of ordered liberty," surely it would seem, in such fields, to get us no further than would a quite warrantable inference from the status of citizenship. It is perfectly true that, in some times and places, perhaps in most times and places, the status of citizenship would not have implied immunity from religious coercion. But in those times and places, equally, neither the phrase "due process of law" nor the concept of "ordered liberty" would have seemed to suggest such an immunity. I may add, warning you that I am far from being an historian, that I know of nothing in our history to contradict the hypothesis, which seems to be suggested by Professor Howe's historical discussion, that full and free participation in our polity has always in fact entailed immunity from coercion or near-coercion in religious matters.

I am led, by the concept of ordered liberty and of the right to live under such a regime as an inference from the status of citizenship, to the field of criminal procedure. I am going to take this field up in another connection tomorrow. Let me just now say, however, as time is so short, that it seems to me that an inference of immunity from arbitrary arrest, oppressive interrogation, unfair trial, and the like might easily have been drawn from the status of citizenship, once the decision had been taken to look on that status as more than the right to a label. But I will leave it with that, particularly since the textual warrant in the due process clause is so firm as to all these procedural matters.

I shall now redeem my promise to say something about aliens. There is little question that judicial reluctance to employ the privileges and immunities clause as a ground for decision has stemmed in part from the fact that that clause protects only citizens. The same reluctance, judicial and extrajudicial, must arise when one puts forward any line of reasoning based on the sheer status of citizenship. To this I would reply, shortly, that there seems to me few relational inferences better warranted than the inference that the national power over aliens as such is paramount, and that the states may not in general take any action against them as aliens. They are admitted by Congress. They reside where Congress (subject in this, as in all other matters, to such constitutional restrictions as Congress is under) says they are to reside. They stay here by national permission, on such terms as the nation imposes, or chooses not to impose. They are to be naturalized when and as Congress prescribes. Our relations with them vitally concern our foreign relations and our foreign commerce. That states may refuse them certain political privileges reasonably to be reserved for residents of more certain permanency and attachment, such as voting, may consist with their dominant relation with the national government. But that relation seems to me an entirely satisfactory ground for a general doctrine of national constitutional preemption, when it comes to most state discriminations against them.

Now I started tonight by blotting out of the Constitution fifty-two words—those words in the Fourteenth Amendment which we look to for virtually all our protection against the exertion of state power against individuals in such a manner as to impair freedoms important to the nation. My general submission has been that we would not have been quite at sea if those words had never been inserted in the Constitution. Doctrines and results would have been somewhat different, for better or for worse. But it seems to me that, in the status of the national citizen (and even of the lawful inhabitant) as political participant, as warranted claimant to membership in the public life, as free man, there might have been found much the same immunities as those we have perilously worked out from the fifty-two word text. The inferences would have been bold; they would often have rested on assessment of the weight of competing arguments rather than on demonstration. But who on earth would say anything other than that of the process by which the thirty-one words of the due process and equal protection clauses were brought to do the work they have done? Is it not through such bold assessments of the weight of competing considerations that all law has always built its systems, worked toward its goals?

Of course our legal culture will not change its spots, and we will go on relying, by and large, on those fifty-two or thirty-one words. But I would think we could do so with more confidence if we had the feeling that, after all, it was not mere textual accident in 1866 that made all the difference—that there was more to be said, even in law, for free speech and racial freedom than that the words of the Fourteenth Amendment commanded them—that our most precious freedoms may with good show of reason be thought to have even deeper foundation, in our political system and in our guaranteed enjoyment of citizenship. And I should hope that when some emergent problem might be solved by these means, we may show at least enough methodological flexibility to take a long look at this way to solution.

III · Constitutional Structure and Judicial Review

In the two preceding lectures, I have explored with you a few of the substantive implications which I believe can be discerned in the structural relations of nation, states, and people. This afternoon I want to finish by raising some questions about the impact of structural considerations on the practice of judicial review.

Our Supreme Court is a component in a political structure, interacting with all the other components. In the main, since it is a court, its mode of interaction with other parts of government is that of interpretation and execution of expressed policies formed elsewhere. Professor Max Gluckman, in his recent insightful exploration of Barotse legal ideas, has shown that the officer whose function it is to execute the policy of a superior inevitably acts as a softener, a deflector, a transformer of that policy.[1] The circuit is not passively obedient; it has its own inductance, its own resonance, and the policy it transmits bears the mark

[1] THE IDEAS IN BAROTSE JURISPRUDENCE, *passim*, but especially p. 42 (1965).

of these as well as—and sometimes in spite of—the incoming signal. Students of the interpretation of legislation by judges will have no difficulty in furnishing Professor Gluckman with instances. Judges are in this sense in perpetual confrontation with the authority they are institutionally bound to obey. This is not a result of their own waywardness, but rather inheres in the nature of things, at least in the range from Northern Rhodesia to New Haven.

But when we come to the distinctively American institution of judicial review for constitutionality, we have to deal with a different and far more conscious and explicit kind of confrontation. The judicial officer is now appealed to not merely to do what all judicial officers everywhere, and all executants of general policy everywhere, do by necessity. He is being called on to overrule in terms the action of some other political authority.

Judicial review for constitutionality does not present the only occasion for explicit judicial overruling of the decision of some other political authority. Judges at all levels are continually performing this function. The actions of municipalities are annulled as being in violation of the provisions of the city charter passed by the legislature. A governor's action, purporting to be taken under a state statute, may be struck down as violating that statute. An administrative board may be held to have exceeded the powers granted it by Congress. Judicial business like this is exceedingly common. Nor is it always easy to state, for the general case, a clear political difference between this kind of review and review for constitutionality. In a state with an easily amendable and frequently amended constitution, like California's, judicial annulment of a state statute on state constitutional grounds is really no more than the striking down of one political act in the name of a provision rather easily changeable by another political act.[2]

We put judicial review for federal constitutionality in a different class from all these other kinds of judicial review, partly because we know how difficult it is to amend our federal Constitution, and partly, I should think, for reasons sounding deeper in political symbolism. I want to talk this afternoon about the *kinds* of confrontation in which the ultimate judicial authority, our Supreme Court, may find itself when it exercises this most interesting of its functions. I think I will be defining "confrontation" with sufficient rigor if I say that I mean to explore some possible answers to the questions: Whose action is the Court annulling? Whom is the Court second-guessing? Who, before the Court acts, has made the critical determi-

[2] See *California's Constitutional Amendomania*, 1 Stanford Law Review 279 (1949).

nation which the Court is asked to reverse? Assessment of the political meaning of judicial review for federal constitutionality, in any given range of cases, very much depends on the answer to these questions. Much of what I shall say will have the feel of obviousness, but it is an obviousness often enough disregarded or blurred to make useful its restatement.

The accuracy of our perceptions of the nature of the confrontations found in judicial review for federal constitutionality has been dulled by the intellectual and political fascination of the question posed and answered in *Marbury* v. *Madison*.[3] In that case, Marshall set forth some of the arguments for judicial review involving one special and ultimate confrontation, the confrontation between the Court and Congress, as Congress has expressed itself in the forms set by the Constitution. His arguments for the propriety of the Court's overturning a prior judgment of Congress were not absolutely conclusive—as arguments on either side of such a question rarely if ever can be—though I do not mean, in saying this, to suggest that his arguments, and other arguments he might have chosen to use at that time, were not decidedly weightier than those that might have been brought forward to support the opposite conclusion. The vital thing in 1968 is that as a political matter,

[3] 1 Cranch 137 (1803).

if not as a matter of strict legal theory, judicial review of Acts of Congress for federal constitutionality no longer rests wholly on the arguments of *Marbury* v. *Madison,* or on those of Federalist No. 78, or on any other arguments that might have been urged in early years. It rests also on the visible, active, and long-continued acquiescence of Congress in the Court's performance of this function. The Court now confronts not a neutral Congress nor a Congress bent on using its own constitutional powers to evade the Court's mandates, as some state legislatures have tried (and as Congress very clearly could succeed in doing, in many cases, if it were so minded), but rather a Congress which has accepted, and which by the passage of jurisdictional and other legislation has facilitated, this work of the Court. Even so, there remains undoubtedly a specially heightened interest in this confrontation between the ultimate national representative body, on the one hand, and on the other a Court acting in the name of an all but un-amendable fundamental national law.

Because of this interest, I think, our views of the confrontations in judicial review tend to become skewed. We take note of differences, but then the huge mass of the *Marbury* v. *Madison* question draws us, and we are pulled back to it, forgetting the distinctions observed. I think this can be documented, out of first-class works, even for the last decade. For this purpose, I should like to expand some brief remarks I have recently made elsewhere on this curious skewing. I take examples out of the top drawer; they are always the most interesting ones to talk about.

The late Judge Learned Hand[4] and my colleague Alexander Bickel,[5] have published within the last decade works on judicial review, each taking a set of positions which I, as a judicial activist proudly self-confessed, would identify as passivist in tendency. Each feels the obligation to begin by stating at length his estimate of the legitimacy, the lawfulness, of judicial review. This seems to me a reasonable beginning; our attitude toward an institution may rightly be influenced by our judgment as to the validity of its warrant to existence. One might naturally go slow in exercising a function assumed by mistake and sanctioned only by prescription. Each of these authors discusses in great depth the problems of legitimizing judicial review, but focally in *Marbury* v. *Madison* terms—in terms, that is to say, of review by the Court of Acts of Congress. Then Judge Hand goes forward, apparently unconscious of any anacoluthon, to the canvassing of examples drawn both from the field he

[4] THE BILL OF RIGHTS (1958).
[5] THE LEAST DANGEROUS BRANCH (1962).

has discussed and from the field of judicial review of state actions for their federal constitutionality. Bickel says a few words, indicating summarily that he perceives the problem as much the same, and proceeds to discuss examples similarly mixed.

Now, with great deference (and in the case of Bickel, whom I know, with great affection), that simply will not do. Either it is relevant to modern problems to assess the bedrock legitimacy of judicial review, or it is not. If it is not, let's forget about it altogether. If it is, then the relevance has to be a differentiated relevance; the view one takes of the logic of *Marbury* v. *Madison,* or of the substitutes one discerns for *Marbury* v. *Madison,* cannot be relevant to the attitude one is to assume toward review of the actions of the states for their federal constitutionality. For the modes of legitimation are entirely different. *Marbury* v. *Madison* may be thought to pose a problem—a problem to which the right solution was found, I think, but a problem nonetheless. There simply is no problem about the fundamental legitimacy of judicial review of the actions of the states for federal constitutionality. Article VI says as much, literally and directly. Justice Gibson, the earliest considerable critic of *Marbury* v. *Madison,* in his celebrated opinion in *Eakin* v. *Raub,* saw and said just this, dismissing the subject shortly as completely covered by Article VI.[6] The particular ways in which the federal courts get their hands on questions of this class are in every case prescribed by Congress, and those particular ways have sometimes been attacked as unconstitutional. But in the leading case on this, *Martin* v. *Hunter's Lessee*,[7] which upheld the power of Congress to direct the Supreme Court to hear writs of error to state court judgments denying federal claims under a jurisdictional statute which lumped federal constitutional claims with others, counsel conceded, and it was assumed, that cases involving such federal claims could undoubtedly be brought by Congress under the hand of the federal judiciary; it was only the particular manner of doing so that was under attack. On the whole, there is nothing in our entire governmental structure which has a more leak-proof claim to legitimacy than the function of the courts in reviewing state acts for federal constitutionality. Indeed, as I have said elsewhere, it seems to me Congress could have provided for this even without an Article III, simply by creating a court and endowing it with the power to perform this necessary and proper function.

Insofar, then, as legitimacy in origin is relevant to

[6] 12 S. & R. 330 (1825).
[7] 1 Wheaton 304 (1816).

judicial or public attitude toward the judicial work, the Court ought to feel no slightest embarrassment about its work of reviewing state acts for their federal constitutionality. It seems very clear, moreover, that all present-day political considerations strongly impel toward the same conclusion. In policing the actions of the states for their conformity to federal constitutional guarantees, the Court represents the whole nation, and therefore the whole nation's interest in seeing those guarantees prevail, in their spirit and in their entirety.[8] The Court is in all practical effect the delegate of Congress to do this work.

The great cleavage among confrontations, then, is between these two altogether different types of judicial review. It is very interesting, I think, that virtually all intense political trouble about the Court's role in the last three decades concerns its functioning in the one of these roles whose legitimacy is not so much as fairly debatable. In the casebook out of which I teach constitutional law, there is a list of all the cases, from 1937 to 1967, in which the Court has annulled an Act of Congress.[9] As of the time of going to press, the editors could list just a dozen cases. Not one of these cases, I believe, has created any major political

[8] See *Boyd* v. *United States*, 116 U.S. 616 (1886).

[9] Freund, Sutherland, Howe and Brown, CONSTITUTIONAL LAW: CASES AND OTHER PROBLEMS (3d ed. 1967) p. 24.

furor, any disturbance of public opinion, at all comparable to that engendered by the school prayer and Bible-reading decisions, by the decisions desegregating the state school systems, by the decisions reapportioning the state legislatures, or by the series of decisions imposing more stringent rules on police and prosecutorial conduct—all decisions bearing entirely or in overwhelmingly preponderant part on the states. It would not be too much to say that the Supreme Court in our times is a dangerously controversial institution only as it acts as a principal national institution charged with the duty of bringing the states into line with national law, and that its exercise of the *Marbury* v. *Madison* function, when controversial at all, is so only at a categorically lower range of intensity. Is it not plain that what is chiefly objected to is not the Court as such, but the fact of being brought into line? In any case, the use of discussions of *Marbury* v. *Madison* as a propaedeutic to the evaluation of the Supreme Court's constitutional work in our generation is at best an anachronism, and at worst a seriously misleading suggestion of doubt where no legitimate doubt can exist.

But the inapplicability of *Marbury* v. *Madison*, if one may use a rather comic phrase, is by no means exhausted by pointing to the difference between judicial review of federal actions and judicial review of state actions for their constitutionality. The political and legal problems of *Marbury* v. *Madison* exist in only one kind of confrontation—the confrontation of Congress and the Court. In many cases passing on the constitutionality of federal actions, what is actually involved is a confrontation between the Court and some official to whose judgment on constitutionality none of the piously repeated rules of deference and restraint have anything like the application they might be thought to have to Congress.

The simplest example is a case like *Massiah* v. *United States*. Massiah was out on bail, awaiting trial on a narcotics indictment.[10] Government investigative officers procured the cooperation, as it is called, of one of his co-defendants and installed a radio transmitter in the co-defendant's automobile. Massiah and this co-defendant, sitting in the automobile, had a conversation in the course of which Massiah made self-incriminating statements; needless to say, no lawyer was present. The Court held this evidence inadmissible on the ground that the Fifth and Sixth amendments forbade even the surreptitious taking of statements from an indicted defendant out of the presence of counsel.

I am not concerned with whether you think this decision to have been correct; I am not at all sure

[10] 377 U.S. 201 (1964).

that I do. What I want to point out is that there is no occasion, in such a case, for those incantations of deference and judicial self-doubt which may have some appropriateness when an Act of Congress is under review. The only constitutional judgments made on this investigative technique, before the case came under the judicial hand, were made by investigators and prosecutors. It would, I think, be hard to state a sound political reason for the judicial branch's doing anything but walking into such a case with no presumptions of constitutionality whatever, with no apparatus of judicial self-denial. If the courts do not do that, then Massiah never gets a responsible and competent judgment on the constitutionality of what has been done to him, never gets a judgment from anybody except his formal adversaries in the criminal process. That cannot be right.

Such cases are rather simple. I will go on to mention two problem areas that are more complicated. First, there is the case where Congress, by very broad and vague delegation, puts it within the power of some official to behave in a manner of questionable constitutionality, but does not direct him to behave in the manner which does finally raise the constitutional question. Secondly, there is the case where the confrontation is not with Congress as a constitutional law-making body that has put a challenged law on the statute books, but with some part of Congress, or with some inference drawn from something Congress has done or not done, outside the forms prescribed by the Constitution for Congress's recording its will.

Cases of the first sort fall out in rather bewildering variety, and analysis of them may go in several directions. The Court's typical—and seemingly harmless—solution has been to read the delegation itself as not including the power to tamper with important constitutional rights, so that—on this purportedly statutory ground—the official is held without power to do what he has done. This was the holding in the 1958 case of *Kent* v. *Dulles*, where the action of the Secretary of State in refusing a passport on grounds of Communist affiliation was taken under powers derived from an extremely vague delegation.[11] I have called this method of solution harmless, and it is that, as long as the Court keeps firmly in mind that in such a case it is not confronting Congress at all, and remains institutionally free, and indeed bound, to make its own judgment unembarrassed by presumptions.

Korematsu v. *United States* is a most interesting

[11] 357 U.S. 116 (1958).

case in this context.[12] Korematsu was convicted under an Act of Congress making it a crime to disobey the order of any military commander in any military zone or area, with respect to entering, remaining in, leaving, or committing any act in such a zone. What he really disobeyed was an order by General DeWitt, military commander for California, that all citizens of Japanese ancestry leave certain areas—an order, which, in the light of other orders in effect, required Korematsu to go to a concentration camp. General DeWitt fell within the description of those authorized by the President to issue such orders, in the most general terms. Nobody but General DeWitt had ever taken responsibility for the decision that Japanese-Americans were to be excluded from their West Coast homes and locked up in concentration camps. I digress briefly to say what a shameful thing I think it is either that rabbit-from-the-hat legerdemain of this kind was employed to bring it about that a decision taken at the highest level should be camouflaged so as to appear to be the decision of one General DeWitt, or, equally disgraceful, though I judge far less likely, that it really was wholly left to this worthy general to decide on such a step as the Japanese evacuation and imprisonment program. But

[12] 323 U.S. 214 (1944). See Rostow, *Japanese-American Cases: A Disaster*, 54 Yale Law Journal 489 (1945).

in either case, the point for us here is that there was no genuine confrontation of the judgment of any co-ordinate branch. Congress, by inadvertence or by design, had made and recorded no judgment on racial exclusion from California, or on the whole policy of racial exclusion, or on race as a criterion for any official action. The President, instead of taking specific formal, public responsibility for a step of such solemnity and magnitude, authorized it in terms so general and so vague that no one reading his Executive Order could have dreamt any such thing was afoot. The Court was the very first authority other than General DeWitt to take responsibility for judgment on the constitutional propriety of this whole racial exclusion program; it came under the Court's hand not blessed, in any recognizable way, by any coordinate political authority. Yet the tradition of deference to coordinate political authority makes the Court say: "In the light of the principles we announced in the *Hirabayashi* case, we are unable to conclude that it was beyond the war power of Congress and the Executive to exclude those of Japanese ancestry from the West Coast war area at the time they did." But, as Mr. Justice Jackson, dissenting, said: "But the 'law' which this prisoner is convicted of disregarding is not found in an act of Congress, but in a military order. Neither the Act of Congress nor the Executive Order of the President,

nor both together, would afford a basis for this conviction. It rests on the orders of General DeWitt."

It seems to me that a sound attention to the
problem of actual confrontation might have led the
Court—or two more of its members, and that would
have been enough—to decline a deference to the
authority they actually confronted—General DeWitt
—so great as to allow the judicial branch to be employed to punish a man for violating a racially based
order the necessity and propriety of which was
vouched for only by the general.

Let me pass on to the problem of confrontation
between the Court and parts of Congress.

Preliminarily, let us note that the Constitution
provides one way, and one way only—and that is a
way hedged with careful safeguards—for Congress to
express the national purpose and will. A measure,
embodying law in fixed language suitable for inclusion
in the statute books, may pass both Houses, and then
either be signed by the President or repassed by two-
thirds of each House, on recorded yeas and nays.
When the Court confronts Congress as a constitutional entity, it is because it confronts that kind of
action, of a content such as actually to pronounce on
the problem before the Court, and I think he would
be a frivolous judge indeed in whose mind something

like a presumption of constitutionality would not arise on such an occasion.

But parts of Congress, and more or less clearly evidenced trends in Congress, can be confronted as well. It is my submission that nothing like the same deference is due on these occasions.

There comes to mind here, of course, the celebrated *Barenblatt* case, so often commented upon in this connection.[13] Barenblatt had been called before a subcommittee of the House Un-American Affairs Committee, and had refused to answer its questions. The Court analyzed the case as requiring its decision on the subcommittee's authority to compel testimony, on the pertinency of the questions asked by the subcommittee, and, finally, on the striking of a balance between the associational freedom of Barenblatt and the national needs served by the subcommittee's inquiries. As to all these questions, and particularly as to the last and most crucial, the Court was not confronting Congress at all; the determinations it was being asked to reverse were those of the subcommittee only. It is impossible to say what the result would have been if this had been kept clearly in focus. What is certain is that the "balance" struck by the subcommittee is not seriously inquired into, but is

[13] *Barenblatt* v. *United States*, 360 U.S. 109 (1959).

treated rather as if it were a balance struck by Congress. When the question of motive came up—Barenblatt having charged that the subcommittee's motive was not information but exposure—the Court said:

> Nor can we accept the further contention that this investigation should not be deemed to have been in furtherance of a legislative purpose because the true objective of the Committee and of the Congress was purely "exposure." So long as Congress acts in pursuance of its constitutional power, the Judiciary lacks authority to intervene on the basis of the motives which spurred the exercise of that power.

Note how the subcommittee—the only directly relevant body—never appears in this formulation, and even the committee drops out of sight in its second sentence. I cannot say, of course, that there would have been a different result if the Court had kept the exact nature of the confrontation clearly in mind. I do say that the perception by the Court of the part it is playing in the governmental machine, in any particular case, must necessarily have some effect on its approach in marginal cases, and that nothing but gain can come from its keeping itself sharply aware of these differentiations, while nothing but loss can come from their blurring.

I do not know whether the Adam Clayton Powell

case will ever come under the hand of the Court.[14] But if it does it would be utterly false to view it in *Marbury* v. *Madison* terms, as a clash between the Court and Congress. One House of Congress, in an adjudicatory rather than in a legislative capacity, has acted under a view of its own constitutional powers which is supported by no action of either of the components —the Senate or the Presidency—whose concurrence is necessary in the legislative process that fixes national policy. The action is one of deep interest to the whole nation, and not merely to the House. There may be reasons for the Court's regarding such an action as unexaminable by the judiciary, or as entitled to deference, but they cannot be the same reasons as those which would be invoked in the case of an action by Congress as a whole constitutional body.

The blurring of these distinctions runs through a considerable body of legal discourse. I think of Mr. Justice Harlan's dissent in *Wesberry* v. *Sanders*.[15] That case, as you recall, concerned the subject of unequal apportionment of congressional districts. The Court held that a requirement of equality in such districting was a fair inference from Article I of the Con-

[14] See Eckhardt, *The Adam Clayton Powell Case*, 45 Texas Law Review 1205 (1967).
[15] 376 U.S. 1 (1964).

stitution. I am not concerned now with overall evaluation of that holding. I would call attention only to a part of Mr. Justice Harlan's dissent. He attacks the Court's holding as flying in the face of Congress's own action. But that action was not a positive declaration by Congress; it was rather the striking out, by the House of Representatives, of a requirement of district population equality, in a 1929 act providing machinery for the apportionment of representatives among the states. The action of the House was taken, as far as the meager debate shows, on vague and self-contradictory grounds; there is even reason to think that some members thought the omitted requirement was unnecessary, since it would in any case continue as part of the standing law.[16] The question never came into any kind of focus, however blurred, in the Senate, nor is there the slightest evidence that the President in signing the bill ever considered or had any notice, constructive or actual, that he ought to consider a possible negative inference from the absence of such a provision, in an act whose weight lay quite elsewhere. Yet Mr. Justice Harlan says that the Court is "over-ruling congressional judgment."

If so ambiguous an action by Congress as that of

[16] The material is summarized in my *Inequities in Districting for Congress*, 72 Yale Law Journal 13, on pp. 18–21 (1962).

failing to state, in a bill concerning another subject, a requirement of district equality is coolly to be treated as tantamount to the passage by Congress (in the prescribed constitutional manner), of a law declaring that inequality in districts is to be permitted, then what use is there in the constitutional prescription of procedures by which law is to be made and published? The Court in *Wesberry* was not in confrontation with any constitutional action of Congress, but with a cloudy innuendo, a doubtful guess as to how Congress —that is, the House, the Senate, and the President in their constitutionally prescribed coaction—would have acted on a definite declaration, to be printed in the statutes at large, affirmatively sanctioning congressional malapportionment. The legislative history very certainly does not answer this question, and as long as it does not, Mr. Justice Harlan's imagination of prior action by Congress is the reverse of clarifying.

Now let me turn again to the problem of judicial review of state actions for their federal constitutionality and remind you that all these distinctions subsist as well in that field as in the federal-on-federal kind of review. I have said that review of the act of a state legislature ought not to invoke the kind of judicial deference suitable where the act of the coordinate and national body—Congress—is under examination. Still, the fully formal action of a state legislature has a considerable weight; it represents the best and most authentic judgment of the state as a political body. But a great deal of the review performed by the Court —most of it, probably—does not concern such acts at all, but rather places the Court in confrontation with minor state officialdom.

I am going to deal with only one very general kind of this confrontation, but it is one of vast importance. I hark back to my previous discussion of the *Massiah* case. That case involved judicial disapproval of an investigative method used by federal officers. But one of the most important branches of judicial review today involves federal judicial annulment of state criminal convictions on the ground of the unconstitutionality of the practices of state or local police.

I would strongly suggest that the confrontation problem is absolutely crucial here. The issue, basically, is whether due process of law is afforded when some investigative technique is employed, such as (in the celebrated *Miranda* case) police interrogation without counsel.[17] But in the overwhelming majority of such cases the only extrajudicial determination of the propriety or constitutionality of the conduct concerned is that of the police. There is, of course, a state judicial ruling on the federal constitutional claim, but nobody has ever suggested that such a ruling is not reviewable

[17] *Miranda* v. *Arizona*, 384 U.S. 436 (1966).

by the Supreme Court without embarrassment. Outside the court system, the authority the judiciary confronts is not Congress, not the legislature, not the governor, not even the city council, but Chief Doe. If Chief Doe did not in good faith consider the federal constitutional problem, his judgment on it is nonexistent. If he did consider it, his judgment, I think it not too unkind to say, is worthless. When the accused person appeals to the Court on the federal constitutional ground, he is appealing to the very first official authorized or competent—or for that matter, likely—to consider his claim.

I think that *that* is what is most fundamentally wrong with such situations as those the *Miranda* case sets out to correct. We are taken all the way back to the Magna Charta conception of procedure according to the *law* of the land, a concept with which the Edwardian "due process" formula is commonly equated. In the great majority of instances, investigative practices have grown up and established themselves without any formal sanction at all from anybody authorized to state or establish the law of the land. In my view, this is the most fundamental possible want of due process. A suspect is subjected to drastic treatment, but the legislatures and Congress have simply looked the other way, and taken no responsibility for striking the balance between the claims involved. If judicial respect for the legislative branch's findings and determinations is to make a difference, then surely it must make a difference that there is no occasion, in most of these cases, for such respect, because the legislative branch has studiously abstained from dealing with the problems.

These considerations explain to me, as they have to others, a good deal of the Court's recent activism in the criminal procedure field. That activism seems to me wholly justified, not necessarily because every one of the practices under review is evidently intrinsically wrong, but because due process of law ought to be held to require an active judgment by the legislative branch, rather than by the police chief, on how much of our personal liberty and security we must surrender in the interest of a practicable administration of the criminal law. One cannot prove what might have been the result of a contrary-to-fact condition in the past, but I shall always think that the problems presented would have had a different aspect, and the solutions a different tenor and tone, if the Court had confronted thoughtfully drawn state or national codes, enacted by the responsible legislative bodies, instead of raw actions by the police.

If this line of thought has validity, then it would seem to be by no means too late. If a major way in which due process of law was wanting—in, say, the

Miranda case—lay in the want of any law at all governing police conduct, then a good faith change in that regard might contribute to solving some of the problems said to be created by decisions of the *Miranda* type. There is some language in the *Miranda* opinion which might encourage that hope. That language may well be worth following up.

In *Stoner* v. *California,* in 1964, the Court held the search of a hotel room unlawful, where the only justification urged was that the night clerk had given permission.[18] Mr. Justice Stewart, writing for a Court unanimous on the main point involved, said something which may indicate an awareness of the issue I am talking about here. "Even if it be assumed that a state law which gave a hotel proprietor blanket authority to authorize the police to search the rooms of the hotel's guests could survive constitutional challenge, there is no intimation that . . . California has any such law." I do not mean to say that it is my view that in Stoner the existence of such a law would have made a difference. I mean only to say that this sentence is of high interest, as showing an awareness by the Court of the different substantive issue tendered by a police decision on the one hand, and a legislative decision on the other, when what you are looking for is "due process of law."

[18] 376 U.S. 483 (1964).

I can easily imagine a scheme of thought in which investigative procedures might be judged in a frame of reference more finely graded than the present. Some practices, beyond doubt, would be unconstitutional at all events. Others might be of such character that a state legislature might authorize them. Others, more seriously affecting the individual, might have to be authorized by Congress. I venture to guess that even now, if Congress, acting under the clear warrant of its section five power to enforce the Fourteenth Amendment, carefully defined the limits of police practice, and then put federal teeth in the rule that those limits might not be transgressed, the Court would very seriously respect and in large measure defer to this expression by the national legislature on national need, and on national interpretation of the due process clause.

I have spoken of the *Miranda* case and similar decisions not as a student of the criminal law process, but as a constitutional lawyer, considering not the needs of police interrogation, of which I know nothing, but the structural factors which might still make a solution possible, if a serious problem does exist. It has been thought by some that the game is really over— that *Miranda*, for example, has "constitutionalized" the rule that no suspect may be interrogated at any stage for any length of time without counsel. I submit that all *Miranda* need be held irrevocably to have constitutionalized is the rule that this may not be done where the highest relevant policy-forming authority in respect of the enforcement of the Fourteenth Amendment has never recorded any judgment in the matter. We do not judge the constitutionality of punishment solely on the basis of whether the conduct punished might constitutionally be made punishable; we require responsible determination by someone other than police and prosecutors that it is to be punishable. There is no reason why something of the sort might not apply to those drastic invasions of personal liberty which we are now told are necessary in the investigative process.

As I think back over what I have said in these lectures, I realize that the most I can hope for is that I may have suggested some lines along which some of you may later find it fruitful to think. One who reads at all in constitutional law will know, ruefully, that there is no new thing to be said, and that when you think you have said something new you later find that others have said much the same thing before. Still, I think it is right that the method of inference from structures, status, and relationship is relatively little attended to in our legal culture, and even if I buy a pocket book in the station in New Orleans and read on the way home almost everything I have said here,

I shall not be sorry for having raised some of these problems in your minds.

As to substance, I think the method of inference from structure and relation has several interesting things about it. Probably the chief interest is sheerly intellectual; it is fascinating to me to speculate on how far we might have gone along these lines if this had been the method of choice in our tradition. Of course, as I pointed out yesterday, not every step we would have taken would have been absolutely compelled logically—far from it. But that, emphatically, is true of the great and small progressions of every legal method. There would have been more judgment than logic, more weighing than mathematics, in a rounded development, covering all problems, of a theory of free speech based not on text but on political relations; but that is true of the method of textual interpretation too, and surely is true of the common law, where development through the cases very visibly takes directions not compelled but merely left open by formal reasoning. At all events, it is interesting to guess what might have been.

Secondly, in some fields, I think the judgments that have been made on the basis of exegesis of text may be firmed up, and doubts about them dispelled, by reflections on this alternative method. I think this comment is more conspicuously applicable in the field of protection against state interference with free speech than in any others I have touched on. There has remained, I think, a suppressed uneasiness about the incorporation of the First Amendment into the Fourteenth—suppressed because it came to seem so unthinkable that there could be no federal protection of free speech against local interference, but an uneasiness because the conversion of the phrase "due process of law" into a statement of preferred position must continue to be suspected of being arbitrary. For the reasons I gave last night, I for one am convinced that sound law, without any supporting text, ought always to have seen state interference with utterance, on a broadly defined range of topics connected with possible national political activity, as sweepingly forbidden; this conviction, for those who share it, must dispel much of the uneasiness.

Then, too (and I say this because of a consciousness, from long experience, that no legal argument seems equally forceful to all men of equal acumen) it may be that a line of thought based on relation, status, or structure may fail to convince some mind, strictly as a matter of law, and still play a part in the formation of attitude toward law. Here I think of the derivation, to which I have referred, of Negro rights from the status of citizenship. I am sure that some to whom this line of argument will not seem as independently convincing as it does to me will nevertheless think it helpful and suggestive when it comes to the formation of political attitudes toward racism, and even when it comes to forming a set of mind toward the interpretation of the equal protection clause.

Thirdly, I think there do occur problems which quite definitely ought to be analyzed in terms of structure and relation—where that is the one way to clarity and to sound justification of the result. I started with the case of *Carrington* v. *Rash*—the soldier voting case—because it seems to me to be such a case.[19]

Now when it comes to judicial review, and to the problem of confrontation which I have discussed today, I think the utility of precision in these matters is beyond question. A great part of the literature about judicial review deals with the problem of its supposed contradiction to democracy—which inevitably involves the question whether the authority whose act it is annulling has the highest or less than the highest, the directest or less than the directest, warrant to represent the people. Another part of the literature deals with the connected problem of deference to the political branches with their greater expertness—which necessarily raises the question of the claims to deference of the authority actually being second-guessed. It would seem that a call for exact and accurate at-

[19] 380 U.S. 89 (1965).

tention to these matters ought to be wholly unnecessary, but my reading of the literature and of the opinions convinces me that just the opposite is the case.

Let me close with a little epilogue, saying how pleased and honored I am to have received this invitation. I am honored by the compliment conferred by your faculties, but I am also honored to have spoken in a series bearing the name of the late Chief Justice. As you may have gathered, from these talks or from matter *aliunde*, I am somewhat obsessed with the subject of racism. Now I dare say that the Chief Justice and I, had our lives overlapped more than they did, and had we chanced to meet, might have found some points of difference between us on the race question. But when I look back on the long course of judicial decision in this field, it seems to me the tide visibly turned in the days when he presided over the court. The turning is visible in two cases. In *Buchanan* v. *Warley*,[20] in 1917, a unanimous court, presided over by Mr. Chief Justice White, said to those who would set up residential segregation, block by block, by law, "No, that is too much, that goes too far." And two years earlier, the Chief Justice himself, in *Guinn* v. *United States*,[21] took a look at the Oklahoma grandfather clause, and said, in effect: "This palpable

[20] 245 U.S. 60 (1917).
[21] 238 U.S. 347 (1915).

fraud, in furtherance of racism, will not do." The days of joyful acquiescence in whatever might be devised to hurt the Negro ended with those two decisions. The long climb upward, I think, began just with those two cases, and honor should be given where honor is due.